I, WIN

Hope and Life
my journey as a disabled woman
living in a non-disabled world

WIN KELLY CHARLES

with LINELLE

DEDICATION

I would like to dedicate this book
to my amazing parents and my family
who taught me from day one to have
a fighting spirit about having cerebral palsy,
and who never gave up on me.
I wrote this book especially
in honor of an amazing mother.

CONTENTS

Introduction   1

1   My Family – the Power of Unconditional Love   6

2   Standing Still with CP   18

3   Growing up in Aspen   34

4   Living with a Disability in a Normal World   45

5   Attending College   52

6   Working with a Disability   61

7   Keeping a Disabled Superwoman Healthy   67

8   Today   70

Introduction

Many people are surprised when they see my portraits of crystal-blue seas, flowers drenched in fiery hues, and animals that look like they could leap from the frame right into your lap. They assume that an artist with a disability paints very dark pictures.

Well, that's not me! I have never painted a dull picture in my life, and I don't think I ever will. Through my story, I will share with you the secret for painting life in bright, bold colors that pulse with hope.

I also want to build a bridge of communication between the able-bodied and the disabled. Every one of us has a disability, whether it's visible or not. For each of us, there is something that binds the heart a little and makes life a struggle. No matter what that something is for you, we need each other and we can learn from each other.

My disability just happens to be visible. I was born with cerebral palsy, a kind of brain injury which usually occurs at birth, and can affect many parts of the body. In my case, it primarily affects muscle coordination and speech.

Some people only ever see the outer shell of others, so they think I must be deaf, blind, or mentally deficient, right? None of the above! Being ridiculed and discounted could have been very painful for me, except for a feisty and courageous mother. Mom taught me that I could do anything and overcome everything.

She was right to do so, because I now have pretty good "creds" for overcoming long odds. The spinal surgery I had in 2006 was meant to improve my mobility, but it actually left me worse off than I was before.

Then in 2010 Mom passed away from a brain aneurysm. She had been my rock, my caregiver, the person I called "my second brain."

At that point, few people would have gambled money on my future, and I wasn't even 24 years old.

So I'm not going to kid you that life is a big sunshine factory. My challenges have led me down some intensely dark alleys. But I've learned that if you keep moving forward, the shadowed roads are only part of the journey. If you refuse to stop, the shadows are no more than passing scenery. Whatever you do, don't stop! Keep seeking and keep trying, and you will emerge on the other side.

I know this is true, because the two darkest times in my life – they were catastrophic, without exaggeration – have taken me to my greatest joys and accomplishments.

The first catastrophe was the back surgery that failed in 2006. As much as anybody can look forward to surgery, I did. I was 18 years old, and my spine was already curling up like a clenched fist. Over time, this scoliosis could create pressure on my internal organs and also take away my ability to walk. Doctors said that surgery could bring me more freedom. It would be truly life changing.

But the odds were against me. I had an allergic reaction to the anesthesia, and for 20 minutes, my spine went "dead" on the operating table. Now I cannot get around without using a walker. The much-anticipated surgery certainly changed my life... it took away my independent mobility.

First there was the major-league depression. Then came the anger. My mother had always encouraged me to be independent and to work things out for myself whenever I could. She must have held back a bit, to see how I would handle this crisis.

When the physical therapist suggested that I see a psychotherapist, Mom said, "That's enough. Do the physical therapy, Win, but don't talk to her any more about how you feel." Mom always had faith in my abilities. She told me, "Win, I know you can solve this on your own."

That day when we got home, I went on the Internet and found a digital art program that I could download. As a kid I'd always loved art, so it didn't take long to realize that this passion had never left me.

Within a year I had started Aspen Rose Arts, which today is a thriving business. I sell my digital art creations all over the world. Cards, portraits, T-shirts, mugs. I might lack physical mobility, but there is nothing I can't do in the art world! (To see my work, just Google "Aspen Rose Arts.")

Unlike the back surgery, the second catastrophe was completely unexpected. In late July 2010, my mom suddenly complained of not feeling well. She said she had an upset stomach. She never complained of a headache. Soon after we got her airlifted to a hospital, she passed away. It was August 12th. The void inside me was indescribable.

My mother had overflowed with energy and adventure. She was born and raised in Nassau, the Bahamas, and that put a global skip in her step that she passed on to me. She taught me that having cerebral palsy was no reason to slow down or not have adventures.

Yes, cerebral palsy is a challenge, but CP isn't who I am. It does not define me.

Mom made sure that the Bahamas became a second home for me, and that her family was my family. She literally opened up the world to me as we cruised and jaunted all over the globe, from Canada to Russia.

In fact, I owe my very existence to her sense of fun and impulsiveness. One year in the mid-1970s she decided to vacation in Aspen, Colorado. You can guess who was running an audio business there. When they met, Mom was already a world traveler, so after they married, Aspen became her home, too, and he became my dad.

So I grew up at one of the most privileged addresses on the planet. Given all the physical limitations I have, some people find that ironic. They wonder what problems anyone could possibly have in a Mecca of money, easy living, and celebrities. And they would be amazed if they knew the reality.

The truth is, Aspen is like anywhere else, because human nature isn't bound by area code or ZIP code. I grew up expecting to hear some nasty jokes and face rude stares just about every day.

"You know why they act like that, don't you?" Mom would say. "They're afraid of the unknown. Fear is *their* disability."

When my mother died, I lost that wise teacher. She always believed there should be better communication between the disabled and the able-bodied, and she encouraged me to become a liaison. And that was already underway when she died. By 2010, Aspen Rose Arts had become a bridge and a place of understanding, where a disabled artist (me) could communicate effectively and bring beauty to the able-bodied world. But without my most inspiring teacher to guide me, I wondered what more I could do now.

Three months after Mom's passing, that question was answered. In November 2010, I was asked by a dear friend to join a new non-profit organization called Valley Life For All. Our mission is to find appropriate social service assistance programs for disabled persons and senior citizens who live in the Roaring Fork Valley.

Today I'm the organization's vice president and something of a poster child. With a ten-member board of directors, we estimate there are at least 500 people – and probably more – who need help in finding the right programs for their needs.

Losing my mother was truly a catastrophe. But it also led me to write this book. In telling my story, I am honoring her. She taught me not to be intimidated by life, to keep moving through the dark times, and to paint life on a bright bold canvas.

As you hear my story, I hope it inspires you to paint your own life in whatever bold colors best fit you.

**

Chapter 1

My Family – the Power of Unconditional Love

"I want out, *right now*. C'mon, let's get this done!"

That could have been me speaking. From my first moments of existence, right to the present day, if I didn't get my way, I took matters into my own hands. The problem was, the first time I expressed my point of view I was still in the womb. And boy, did I cause a crisis!

The June day I was born in 1987, my mom had stopped at a friend's house. While she was there, she said it felt like she was having mild contractions. But I wasn't supposed to be born yet, not for several months. She shrugged off the discomfort. My mother never babied anyone, not herself and certainly not a pregnancy. Even though she was 35 at the time and I was her first, it was just like her to figure that she could handle it all without help.

Her friend thought differently. 'Hey, Carolanne," she said, "You better get to the hospital. I think Win's coming now!"

Mom's friend was right. They raced to the hospital, and got there just in time to see me come into the world. At one pound 12 ounces, I still hold the record for being the smallest kid ever born at Aspen Valley Hospital. Jan Kennaugh, the doctor who would continue as my doctor and to this day is still my friend, believed that my very premature birth was the most likely cause of the cerebral palsy.

However, the CP diagnosis came later. The first crisis was to stabilize me and get me on track to a "fighting weight." At less than two pounds, I was in crisis. In order to have a fighting chance at life, I needed to quickly gain weight.

Aspen Valley Hospital didn't have the resources to help me, so my parents decided to have me airlifted to Children's Hospital in Denver. On a map, Colorado's capital is just inches away, but when you're in a hurry in the Rocky Mountains, the journey between Aspen and Denver is by air. Or you can count on a drive of almost four hours, and that will include some mountain passes over 10,000 feet in elevation.

Either way, it wasn't like bopping over to the local emergency room. That airlift to Denver was my first experience of challenge and adventure, all in the first few days of life. Even after the airlift, there was no easy journey. When I left Children's Hospital in Denver, I was already six months old.

To this day I sometimes wonder if my parents had any idea of what they were in for. A critical time for me was "step up to the plate" time for them. Maybe that was the first lesson for all three of us. Every one of us is meant to find the blessings in the biggest challenges, no matter what those challenges are.

Sure, if I had a choice, I would not have consciously chosen cerebral palsy, but that doesn't mean that it hasn't brought me blessings. Yes, I really do want to show you how my life has grown and expanded, even in the grip of this physical disability. You, too, can find the blessings underneath the biggest negatives, if you only look for them.

For one thing, CP has forced me to look around with acute awareness. Given my "C'mon, let's get it done yesterday!" brand of impatience, if I hadn't been slowed down by physical limitations, maybe I would have roared right past my true creativity. In the rush, I might have ignored the talent that would make me most happy. Rather than having a constant focus on what I *can't* do, I have found real happiness in creating art, as well as in motivating people who also face huge challenges in their lives.

Because my parents had to deal with a very real survival issue – would I even live long enough for them to celebrate my first birthday? – I learned very early to appreciate my family. When I came into this world, I was already in full crisis mode. A legion of medical personnel was required. It's on the record from day one how much my parents fought for me to live.

I wouldn't know until I was much older all that they went through. Those deeply worrisome early days of my life revealed my parents' true qualities. I handed them a crisis, and they came through with flying colors and an awesome show of strength and love.

That's why I like to joke that God blessed me with cerebral palsy. It's true that my family had the financial and physical resources to take care of me no matter how big or small my needs might be. But more importantly, they had resources of the heart, too.

In other words, from the very beginning, my family loved me, and I have been truly blessed to always know that.

Some people might argue with me. "Sure, if we had the money your parents have, we could have coped, too." It's definitely true that money helped my parents care for me, but hardship comes in all kinds of packages.

For my parents, the choice to love me didn't depend on whether they had money, but it did have another very important impact, namely, what their choice would do to a lifestyle of freedom.

You see, until I came along, they were the complete masters of their own lives. They ran businesses and made daily decisions that other people carried out. Both of them had chosen work that was fun and absorbing, and when their work was done, they had all of Aspen to enjoy, and many friends to enjoy it with them.

Once I came on scene, everything changed. I cannot imagine all the hours and all the days my mother and my father waited in drab hospital rooms, being ushered in and out of impersonal intensive care units, just so they could be with me. My parents were used to directing businesses, making decisions and plans. Now they had to wait until doctors told them what had to be done. The carefree life they had enjoyed for years was over, at least for a while.

I think of the hours my parents spent in Denver, away from our Aspen home, as they prayed and waited for calls from the operating room. For every surgery I had to undergo, my family always had the determination to see me through.

And I know why Mom and Dad were so willing to bet on the long shot that I was. It's because for them, finding each other was a long shot, too.

From Ocean Paradise To Mountain Resort

Most people love to vacation in the Bahamas. But my mother, Carolanne Crothers, couldn't wait to move from the Bahamas to somewhere else. Carolanne grew up in Nassau, where her father headed the regional offices of Caterpillar, Inc., one of the largest construction and mining equipment and engineering services companies in the world. Lots of people would be content to be from a wealthy family and live in a great tourist spot. As one gushing travel guide put it, "The Bahamas offer a distinct blend of international glamour and tropical ease."

But ease and comfort weren't my mother's things. She wanted to improve her life, and to do that, she had to keep moving forward. My grandmother Win (whom I'm named after) has the same drive and ambition, and that makes them both my heroes, for sure.

From her parents, Mom inherited double doses of overachiever DNA. Luckily for me, that was exactly what she would later teach me about. Despite all my challenges and setbacks, and no matter what the obstacles were, Mom taught me to strive for the best.

By telling my story, I hope to show others how to do that, too.

Anyway, at the age of 25, restless and wanting more, Mom decided that moving to the United States was her best shot at creating a full vibrant life for herself. If she could get off the island, she figured she'd have so many more opportunities to expand her creative and business talents.

In that restless frame of mind, she got in touch with several friends she had gone to college with in Atlanta, Georgia. Her friends were then living in Aspen, Colorado, and they invited her to come for a visit.

And that's how Mom went from growing up in an ocean paradise to settling down in one of the world's greatest mountain resorts.

One night Mom's friends took her to the J-Bar, a legend on the Aspen scene, along with the Hotel Jerome itself. That night she met Tim Charles who had a high-end audio and video company. His family was from Boston and New York. He came to Aspen in 1972 after he graduated from Georgetown University.

In the same way that Mom wanted to leave Nassau and seek a well-rounded life, Dad wanted to get away from East Coast structure and tradition, and find a freer life out west.

Now I wonder. What if Mom and Dad hadn't met? Would Carolanne have finished that Aspen vacation and moved on to explore other places? Or would she have found a job in Aspen and stayed around for a while? Who knows?

The reality is that Carolanne and Tim did meet, and she stayed in Aspen.

My mother found what she had dreamed of. Life with Tim in a legendary mountain town really did expand her world. In Aspen she became the owner of two well-known shops which specialized in fine gold and silver jewelry. She opened Magnolia's first, then later she bought a second shop, and she managed both with flair.

Some people wondered how Carolanne got done in one day everything that had to be done. It was just part of her personality. She drove herself and stayed on top of whatever she was doing. She always followed every project to completion.

So it's no wonder that when I came along, she used the same life principles to guide me and to spur me on to do my very best, even during the darkest days of my life.

Somebody New On The Scene

But even Mom had no clue that one of her biggest adventures was going to be me! After she and Dad met, their lives meshed together harmoniously. Throughout their 20s and into their 30s, Mom and Dad lived much like the motivated, educated, carefree go-getters they were. No, make that *childfree* go-getters.

They enjoyed all the perks of being young successful entrepreneurs in a glamorous resort town. They counted many celebrities among their friends and clients. Dad opened his own audio equipment business and specialized in the installation of high-end audio systems. He offered a valuable service in a community with many entertainers and well-known "names" who guarded their privacy and only gave their business to people they trusted.

Meanwhile, Mom's high-end jewelry shops were thriving, and she catered to clients who appreciated and enjoyed the jewelry.

Then I came along.

Now you might think that the news of a newcomer barging into their lives was a real crisis. There was Mom, a successful business owner in a fabulous playground, and now she's going to have a baby!

To be 35 years old and suddenly pregnant for the first time would be a lot for any woman to absorb – or any couple. But now imagine the shock when your whole life is purring along at a comfortable childfree speed, and suddenly you find yourself racing toward an impenetrable wall of baby blankets.

Mom and Dad took the news in stride. For Mom, the choice was immediately clear. She gave up the jewelry shops and turned her high intensity personality toward the next great adventure in her life ... being a stay-at-home mom.

I might have been a never-before-seen event in their busy lives, but at every turn, my parents responded as positive thinkers and optimists. That was their frame of mind when I was born in the beautiful Rocky Mountain summer of 1987. Despite the fact that I was born as an extreme premie and had to be airlifted to Denver, my parents had every reason to assume that I would rally, gain weight and strength, and come home sooner rather than later. Life would go on pretty much as it had, only with a new daughter.

Maybe they thought that in later years they would have a harrowing "So glad it's over now!" story to tell ... how scared they were when I was born, how incredibly vulnerable I was, a tiny gasp of life, lying helpless in an incubator.

In later years, it would be a real life adventure story, the "All's well that ends well" sort. Something fun to repeat on every birthday, just before I blew out the candles on the cake. Everybody at the birthday party would nod in sympathy and say, "Wow, that must have been a frightening time!" And someone else would pipe up, "Look at Win now," and we would all laugh and tell other stories.

Things didn't turn out that easy.

At the time, I knew none of it. Yet that early time – long before I became aware of my own existence – is a very important part of this book. One message I'm sharing here is that you can get through *any challenge* when you have the support of unconditional love.

In those early days, before I even knew what my struggle was, my parents were there. Yes, I know that all parents love their children, but not all parents get the real opportunity to love unconditionally the way my parents did. Although my life has many more than the usual challenges, and deeper ones in many ways than most children face, the upside is that I have a very clear picture of what unconditional love looks like.

For some of you, the challenge is not having a strong support system – whether that system is made up of parents, siblings, other relatives, or other caregivers. In the past two years, since my mom's passing, I've come to a huge understanding of this. I know how it feels to lose an anchor. I've had to cope daily without her loving strength.

(But that's getting ahead of my story.)

Children's Hospital was at a minimum a four-hour drive from Aspen, so my parents rented a house in Denver to be near me. They also drove back and forth between Denver and Aspen, to deal with various business matters. It's a tedious trip if you're not doing it for fun like a ski trip. At least once that I heard about when I was older, they were forced to go the distance in a driving snowstorm on the mountain highway.

Of course I was too young to be aware of all that they went through at the time. But I've had the privilege of meeting the wonderful doctor who was there from the beginning. She's still in my life today. Her name is Jan Kennaugh.

Recently I asked Dr. Kennaugh to recall what she could about those early days of my life. I am grateful for her memories, and for all she did for me and my parents.

"I took care of Win when she was a premature baby at Children's Hospital," Dr. Kennaugh wrote. "Since I'm a hospital-based neonatology doctor, I wasn't involved in the subsequent medical care or her CP diagnosis.

"But I can shed some light on her first months. Her parents were unbelievably devoted to her despite her being extremely ill and very premature. She was hooked up to machines in the Neonatal Intensive Care Unit. Her parents were eternally optimistic despite the severe prematurity and the illness. She required a ventilator for a prolonged period; she had bleeding in the brain, which was likely associated with the later diagnosis of cerebral palsy.

"Her mother delighted in buying clothes and toys for Win, and was able to stay in Denver with her for long periods. Her father frequently made the journey from Aspen to be with Win. Both were very involved in her care, and despite some medical setbacks, her parents were determined that she would survive and they would provide the best life for her."

Another Major Blow

But not every doctor was as compassionate as Dr. Kennaugh was, or took the time, as she did, to observe how much Mom and Dad loved me. Shortly after the crisis of my birth had passed and I was stable enough for a more normal life, other doctors had a new shock for my parents.

With very little advance notice, they sat my parents down one day and told them that I had cerebral palsy. The condition is a type of brain injury that occurs during or near birth. It has been well known for many decades, but it's still somewhat mysterious because it can have many causes. Those causes are often difficult to trace.

My record-making birth weight of one pound 12 ounces had probably starved my body of precious oxygen. While I was still hospitalized in Denver, no one could say what the effect of cerebral palsy would be on me as a premie weighing less than two pounds and only thirteen inches long.

The doctors had enough information to hand down what they probably thought was a sad life sentence, but they could not tell my parents how severe that sentence might be. Would I be able to talk? Would I spend my life in a wheelchair? Would I be able to think and to communicate with others?

No one knew the answers yet.

My parents cried. They were already exhausted from the frantic worry and constant travel and from caring for me. Now they learned that the pressure would not be easing up any time soon. Maybe not in a lifetime.

Then the news got worse. One day a herd of doctors bustled in, acting self-important and rushed, as if they had to be somewhere else that was much more important to be.

One doctor delivered the blow in a single breath. "The best thing we can recommend that you do for your daughter is put her in an institution."

Wow! With all that Mom and Dad had already faced, that was the worst. Did doctors mean to abandon my case? Weren't they going to help any more?

First my parents felt insulted, then frightened. Then they got angry.

"Hell, no, we are not putting our daughter in an institution!" Dad shouted. "We're paying you to tell us how to care for her, not to get rid of her!"

Of course the doctors explained that they weren't trying to get rid of me... my parents could visit me whenever they wanted, and their daughter would get much better care in a fine facility with professionals more capable of caring for my needs... blah, blah, blah.

"Forget it," Mom said. "Next?"

There was a hidden treasure in all the official talk. Yes, great and good doctors do exist. The treasure among them that day was Dr. Jan Kennaugh, who to this day is my physician. She fully supported my parents; she gave them hope, and she gave them insights on how we could make a life together as a family.

So we moved forward. Blessings and love were following me, despite all the pressure and the frightening unknowns. Still, the journey was only beginning.

**

Chapter 2

Standing Still with CP

"I want people to really see CP,
as it looks through my eyes."

I look in the mirror. The girl looking back at me has long shiny chestnut-colored hair and wide green eyes, just like Mom. As I look closer, I can almost see Mom, although the face that looks back at me is longer and narrower than hers.

Still, I see a pretty girl who is 100 percent herself, with almond-shaped eyes and arched eyebrows that lots of girls would die to have, and a peaches and cream complexion that morphs into a rosy blush in a Colorado winter.

But the mirror doesn't show everything. As my chin juts forward with determination; it clearly expresses my personality, saying, "Go for it!" But that determined slant to my chin also represents a daily balancing act to hold my neck in place. The balancing stress often leads to aching muscles and shooting pains through my neck.

My long narrow face is not only from family genes, but also from having my head basically squeezed in a ventilator for weeks after I was born. Then too, it's the result of lying on one side for so long when I was a premie. Those negative things are as much part of the girl in the mirror as the green eyes and the healthy complexion.

As I study myself in the mirror, I almost laugh at all the contradictions locked behind that interesting and pretty (if I do say so myself) face. For one thing, ever since I can remember, my mind has raced with ideas and opinions, yet long after most kids my age were chattering like Bahaman parrots, I still couldn't say a word. Maybe that's why I love art so much. Even though I couldn't speak, I could paint pictures in my mind.

As for my dreams and goals for the future, there's a contradiction there, too. If you ask me what I want to do, I'll say that more than anything I'd like to be a ballerina. I notice the elegance and precision of a dancer's movements, the lovely arch of her neck as she lightly soars into the air in the hands of a strong partner. To me, a beautiful ballet duet seems like the ultimate freedom.

Other times, like during the Olympic games, I watch ice skaters, and that's where I want to be, too ... in the arena, skating for the gold. In a wonderful way, I did get close to the Olympic spirit, but I'll save that for telling a little later. Right now, I'll just say that ballet dancer and ice skater are two of my many secret wishes, the "wish I could" dreams. So call me Win the Dreamer – I won't mind.

In physical reality, I lurch along, clumping a metal walker on the ground with each step. Compared to most people, I am as slow as winter molasses, especially since that disastrous surgery in 2006 which destroyed most of my mobility.

Still, I have to say that my upper arm strength is amazing. People lift weights to get rippling biceps, but I find that lifting a metal walker with each step does the trick just as well. My spine isn't straight, which means that my head is forward of my shoulders more than on an ordinary person. That gives me frequent neck pain, and makes my profile jut out a bit, just like a turtle.

In other words, *what I want* is to be known as a talented, good-looking young woman with a lot of drive to succeed and many dreams to pursue. I want all those things to be foremost, to be much more prominent than my turtle-like profile. Yet I constantly have to make accommodation for a rude interloper in my life, namely, cerebral palsy.

On one level, cerebral palsy isn't complicated. It's not a rare genetic mutation or an exotic disease. CP is about as complicated as a blow to the head. Actually, that's exactly what it's like.

Cerebral palsy is a condition caused by a brain injury which occurs near or during birth. The most likely cause for my CP is the fact that I was born so premature, and weighed under two pounds. In such a fragile state, my brain began to bleed. I'm one of about 800,000 American children and adults who live with CP. Every year about 10,000 babies develop the condition. That number has stayed constant since the 1980s, the decade in which I was born.

Whatever causes CP, whether oxygen starvation at birth or a birth trauma, the result is a roll call of neurological problems that changes everything. One minute you're cozy and healthy in the womb, and the next minute Mother Nature has hauled back and thrown you a cruel punch. At you, a helpless little baby.

About Cerebral Palsy

"Many children with cerebral palsy have multiple symptoms with combinations of the various forms. Children with *spastic* cerebral palsy often have a head lag which is representative of *hypotonia*. Children with *choreoathetoid* or *hypotonic* cerebral palsy often have deep tendon reflexes which suggest some *spasticity*. Children with *bilateral spastic* cerebral palsy might also have *dystonic* movements in the limbs affected." [quoted from medicinenet.com.]

[*spastic* = marked by abnormal muscular spasms]

[*hypo* = abnormal deficiency; *tone* = the tension in muscles at rest]

[*choreo* = relating to a nervous disorder marked by uncontrollable and irregular muscle movements; *athetoid* = relating to a nervous disturbance marked by involuntary movements, especially in the extremities]

[*bilateral* = having two sides]

[*dys* = impaired function; *tone* = the tension in muscles at rest]

"The different types are rarely seen as pure clinical forms. More often a child with cerebral palsy has a mixture of symptoms. Nevertheless, in clinical practice the type of cerebral palsy is defined on the basis of the predominant manifestations.

"About ten percent has what is known as a mixed type. Some children have both the tight muscle tone of *spastic* CP and the involuntary movements of *athetoid* CP. This is because they have injuries to two areas of the brain.

"Usually the spasticity is more obvious at first, with involuntary movements increasing when the child is between nine months and three years old. The most common mixed form includes spasticity and athetoid movements...." [quoted from medicinenet.com.]

The CP that I have is called mixed cerebral palsy.

The challenges are different for each person with cerebral palsy. For me, it was as if Mother Nature was handing down a life sentence. "You are a gifted person. You will see the world in your own bright, unique way, and you will want to communicate your inspiration to others. You have been given drive and stamina and a never-give-up spirit. You won't ever be afraid to speak your mind.

"But I'm not letting you off easy. It will take you years to discover your artistry. First you will spend long hours learning to speak. Your drive and determination will be tested to the limit, as you learn to control a body's jerky movements.

"Your personality sparkles like the Fourth of July, but some people will think that you are mentally slow. You will be bursting with a quick wit and lots of opinions, but for many years you will struggle just to speak your mind.

"And by the way," Mother Nature continued, "someday you'll want to climb Mount Elbert with your classmates. You'll do it, too, but every step will be as comfortable as hiking across a rock field while wearing ice skates."

So she said.

But I believe in having the last laugh, even on Mother Nature.

Mom Tells Me How It Is

Some people were surprised that I was already in the 7th grade, but even before that, I was adjusting on my own. Sure, I'd wondered why I was different. From the time I was six years old, I wondered. But whatever challenges I had (and there were lots!), I dealt with them as they came. I didn't need a label to tell me that life was not an easy walk up Mount Elbert.

But for some reason, the day Mom told me that I had cerebral palsy was different. The exact conversation is hard to remember. Maybe I was especially frustrated that day, and it was hard to get the words out. Mom and I share many traits. We're both pretty impatient. We want what we want not just *now* but *yesterday*.

Maybe that day I had a tough time talking with a friend, or maybe some physical activity like a class hike or a dance was more than I could take on at the moment. Maybe I was coming to terms that day with how tough it was to do everything I wanted to do.

Maybe that day I came right out and asked Mom, "What's wrong with me?"

Whatever sparked the conversation, that was the day when Mom felt I was old enough to face life with the tagline, "I have CP."

"Win, honey," she said, "we are so proud of you and the way you tackle life. We know it hasn't been easy, and you have physical challenges that your friends don't have. When your dad and I think of how far you have come since we first saw this tiny premie struggling for life... wow! You are succeeding beyond anything we imagined possible.

"We all have life challenges, but yours are especially tough. Now is probably as good a time as any to put a name on it. Your challenge is called cerebral palsy. You know what, kid? You *are* winning!"

Hmm. Win, the winner. Really?

I was quiet for a while, letting everything sink in. It was one thing to accept that I could not speak or walk with the same effortless ease that my friends did. Or that I was not the most graceful skier in Aspen. (Of course, there *is* a lot of competition here for that spot.) But to put a name on it was something new. "This CP ... it's me."

This interloper in my life now had a name. Maybe that meant that it also had a claim on me. I wasn't sure I liked that. I'd been raised to do anything I wanted to do, and that even included skiing. Until the 2006 surgery-gone-wrong, I had always looked at my life in a certain way, and that way did not include a CP label.

Besides, who likes labels? Mom was free-spirited and independent. She taught me to fight my own battles without falling back on excuses or labels. She wanted me to be confident in me as I am, because I'm wonderful just as I am! No excuses necessary.

I can't recall everything about the conversation that day. But I remember that Mom gave me some details. "When you were born, Win, you had two hemorrhages, one on each side of the brain. One side was worse than the other, but both were pretty bad.

"You were so tiny to begin with, just one pound 12 ounces. And you were only thirteen inches long. Smaller than a doll; a very tiny person I could hold in one hand. Your dad and I were frantic to help you. Our hearts were breaking as we watched you struggle to breathe, when you were hooked up to all those machines and tubes.

"But you know what, Win? Even when it was just you and the machines, you were destined to be a winner. And eventually you did win!"

That day Mom also explained how it took several months before they got a diagnosis of CP. It was many years later that I learned the full extent of my parents' pain. The worst moment was when they were advised to put me in an institution.

Instead, they stood up for me with gusto! When I hear about that, I am glad all over again that I have the same fighting spirit my parents have.

But when I was in the 7th grade, it was enough to have my mom sit down and explain to me what my disability was.

Out of the Trash Can

Oscar the Grouch. Lives in a trash can. Complains a lot.

Boy, did I like Oscar the Grouch.

"Oscar" was the first word I learned to say, *then* I learned to say "mama" and "dada." Even that didn't happen until I was four years old, and by that time, I'd been watching Oscar and the other Sesame Street characters for so long, I felt they were members of my family. Oscar was my favorite, for some reason, maybe because he was one frustrated grouch, and I often felt that way, too.

By age four, most kids are tearing around the house and riding their bikes, and words just fly out of them, as easy as breathing. Me? Like every other kid, I was loaded with energy, but CP had pretty much locked me up inside myself. Just like Oscar in his trash can.

My parents knew that speech was the first key to escaping a black hole. They stopped at nothing to find the right speech therapists for me. Their commitment was so intense that we would travel across the country to visit one particular therapist, "the best in the U.S." My regular speech therapist was in Grand Junction, a two-hour drive that could be longer when it was winter time in the mountains.

When you're a kid, you aren't always as grateful as you could be for the opportunities your parents give you. It took me many years to appreciate the time and effort Mom and Dad spent in unlocking my ability to speak. Talk about *freedom of expression*! That phrase means something very special to me.

But when you're going through it, speech therapy is brutal. It's an awful repetition of simple primary sounds, over and over, again and again. Until you go through it, you don't realize how difficult it is.

What made it worthwhile was the outcome, which was pretty amazing. I was doing no less than rewiring my brain. Cerebral palsy had scrambled together all the links in my brain, as if they were tangled-up electrical cords. It took lots of time and lots of patience to pry apart the much-jumbled speech patterns and straighten them out.

At one point, my parents investigated the artificial-voice technology used by the famous physicist Stephen Hawking. If you've ever heard him being interviewed or if you've watched one of his TV specials, you know something about how it works. He taps out sentences on a keyboard, which translates the words into mechanical speech. Could that work for me?

My parents eventually decided against it. For one thing, the technology necessarily produces a rather artificial sound. But more importantly, I had the ability to improve on my own. In Hawkins's case, the disease (ALS) had taken away the tools of speech, so he had nothing to improve on.

My challenge was completely different. I still had the tools, although they weren't in good shape. My parents thought that with time I could get the tools in working order and could learn natural speech on my own.

We also tried something that was more successful, American Sign Language. I learned it as a child. The idea was that in case my speech problems couldn't be overcome, I could be fluent in the beautiful sign language of the deaf and the hearing impaired.

However, with learning and repetition, my verbal skills improved, and by the age of seven, I was talking fluently. In other words, I could chatter away like every other kid!

I'm still intrigued with American Sign Language. Someday I plan to build on that childhood skill, and master this beautiful communication medium. It would be a wonderful asset to my goal of being a bridge between the able-bodied and the disabled, including those who are hearing impaired.

Another problem I faced was just as monumental. The hamstring muscles in my legs tightened up, making it very difficult and painful to walk. It's a common problem with CP, and can sometimes be helped by surgery. The operation is called a "hamstring release." The surgeon snips the hamstring muscles so they don't pull so tightly.

I had it done in the second grade. It wasn't pleasant to go through, but when you're a kid, you don't ask "Why me?" You just accept things and move forward.

All those four-hour drives to and from Denver for consultations and surgeries really got to us. We had to live with each other on the rides. Given all those trips, going from Colorado's Western Slope experts to the Front Range/Denver ones, to the East Coast experts, I'm sure I played "Win, the Grouch" plenty of times with my parents.

Fortunately they had extreme faith in my future and in me. I'm grateful to them for that, and for teaching me to have faith in myself.

Hi! Can You See Me?

The biggest problem with CP is that I'm usually not seen. As with many disabilities, cerebral palsy can make a person invisible. You have no idea what that feels like until you've been there. That's why I really want you to see me through the pages of my book.

It's hard to take being laughed at and made fun of because your speech is slow, or because your limbs are twisted and bent like a wind-driven tree on the side of a mountain. In reality, though, blatant unkindness and nasty behavior don't often happen today.

In the 21st century, people are pretty enlightened about disabilities. Most people know they don't have to be scared of you just because you're obviously different. Most people don't think you're contagious or possessed by a devil, as people might have thought centuries ago. But that doesn't mean they treat you like everyone else. Too many act as if you aren't even there.

Today I run my own company, Aspen Rose Arts, and I have created a body of artistic work. I also have a role as vice president and spokesperson for a nonprofit organization. Yet people still talk over me or around me as if I'm not there. If I wave and say "Hi," some people are so shocked, they don't know how to respond.

Sometimes I wonder who actually has the disability.

Disabled people have to get used to situations like these. As for me, I want to live by a motto that makes sense to me. "Treat everyone with politeness, even those who are rude to you, not because they are nice, but because *you* are."

But being nice doesn't mean rolling over and silently telling someone "Kick me." Mom was the main person who taught me to fight back. We would be in a store or a restaurant, and the waiter or clerk would say something like, "And what will *she* have?" as if I was the Invisible Woman.

Mom would reply "Why don't you ask her?" Boy, did that set them back! But they were learning, too. Again, that's a big reason I am so passionate about writing this book. I want to expose the blind spots we have about each other, so we can all come to a deeper understanding. And I'm not saying I don't have things to learn, too!

I'll let you in on a secret. To this day, I am very jealous of able-bodied people. You take so much for granted! Not just your ability to easily walk and talk, although sometimes I'm jealous of that, too, but because you are usually left alone. You look so normal that people don't even bother to notice you. That's a real treat, which I bet you don't even think about.

As for me, I know that at the first chance, people will steal looks at me, to figure out what's wrong. At the same time, they'll talk over and around me as if I'm not there. I like to think of myself as a winner, but that's one example of how I just can't win.

Here's another one. I'm also jealous of your freedom. The other day somebody asked me if I could drive a car, and I had to say no. It's not just because of the CP itself, but also because the condition gives me what's called a "high startle" reaction. That means I can't stand loud noises, which are not easy to avoid in heavy traffic.

Still, I grasp at freedom whenever I can. One time I decided to hike up Mount Elbert with my classmates. We were all friends with each other, and I felt very comfortable with them. They waited along the trail for me and my adult caregiver to catch up, and we all encouraged each other.

For those who don't know, Mount Elbert is 14,433 feet in elevation. It's the highest peak in Colorado, and if not for Mount Whitney in California which tops Elbert by 72 feet, it would be the highest in the contiguous United States. It's a real accomplishment for anyone to summit Mount Elbert.

As we headed up, the sky darkened and the wind kicked us around. Coloradoans know that it's downright dangerous to be on a high mountain in a storm, because lightning can pick you off at any moment as easily as a sharpshooter picks off a target. It wasn't that bad yet, but we were pretty sure we wouldn't be having a picnic at the top.

My friends and I were there for each other, as we shouted out encouragements over the wind and through the thin mountain air. Every once in a while a buddy would drop back to see how I was doing. And I sure didn't lack for comments, either. As everybody who knows me realizes, I am rarely at a loss for words, even on a hiking trail more than two miles high!

The whole experience was a day of real endurance, and it reminds me of the wonderful quote by the writer McCallister Dodds: "Real strength is not a condition of one's muscle, but a tenderness in one's spirit."

For me, that really rings true. As a disabled woman, I'm as aware of the condition of my muscles as a body builder is, and I know that what makes each of us strong is something more than physical prowess.

That day on Mount Elbert let me see something I have built on ever since. When the disabled and the able-bodied can know each other and see the world from each other's perspective, the way becomes clearer for understanding and lasting friendships.

The trek up Colorado's highest mountain was a real challenge for all of us. Because cerebral palsy causes poor circulation, I'm ultra-sensitive to cold, and the raw biting wind on that screeching day was excruciating.

Then it started to rain. We were about halfway to the summit when the leader said we had to turn back. I don't think Win the Stubborn would have turned around on her own, so I'm very glad it was rain that kicked us all toward home.

Carrying the Torch

So this is me: a smart good looking young woman who is impatient and talented and happy; has her own business, and represents a nonprofit organization; treasures her friends, loves her family (and dearly misses Mom!), and has a million plans for the future. She also happens to have cerebral palsy. Or as I like to say, "I'm a disabled woman, living a non-disabled life."

I would like to be a bridge between the two worlds – those very different territories that are inhabited by the disabled and the able-bodied.

So as you journey with me through my book, the thing I really want you to understand is that both sides have "disabilities." We all have them, in different forms, whether they are physical oddities, deep mental troughs, or fears that hold us back from connecting with others or doing our best. I truly believe we are meant to learn from each other.

No matter what your unfulfilled goal or dream is, you can learn something from this journey. We're all familiar with TV reality shows such as *Survivor* and *Treasure Island* where a treasure worth millions in gold is hidden under six feet of sand and seaweed. It takes searching and digging to find it.

Well, people have hidden treasures, too. Sometimes it takes lots of digging to uncover the beauty and true riches inside a person. Sometimes the more valuable the treasure, the harder it is to find and the longer it takes.

I hope that able-bodied people will understand that people shouldn't be judged on the basis of slow speech or twisted limbs. Inside every person with a disability is a buried treasure of talents and friendship.

As for the disabled, I want to show you that every challenge you face has just two outcomes: you will either conquer it, or you will make headway over it. Even if your gains seem small (I remember the billion times I practiced vowel sounds in speech therapy!), your achievements will eventually shine. So keep searching and keep digging for that treasure!

For everyone, I want my life story to show that it is always possible to move forward, no matter what the challenge is. Ultimately I win, and you will, too.

On February 2, 2002, I was privileged to celebrate a great win. That year, I had a part in the stirring tradition which opens the modern Olympic Games. Before the XIX Games began in Salt Lake City, Utah, the world was treated to the Olympic Torch Relay, where runners take turns carrying the flaming symbol of international cooperation and friendship to the site of the games. In

2002, I was one of the runners carrying the Olympic torch through Aspen.

What an honor to be nominated one of ten! My assignment was to carry the Olympic torch for a quarter of a mile through town. It weighed only a few pounds, so I figured there wouldn't be a problem. But I was concerned about one thing. At a planning meeting for the torchbearers, I learned that I wasn't the only one.

"OK, I know that you're all worried about dropping the torch," the Olympics representative said, as we all laughed nervously. "You know what? Your adrenaline will be pumping so hard, we will have to pry that torch out of your hands!"

She was right. With everything in me, I held that fiery torch. I turned that quarter-mile run into a true victory lap. Along the roadway, people cheered and clapped. I felt as wonderful as if I was actually skating for the gold in the Olympics.

Later, I bought the actual torch I had carried, and two weeks after that, I bought the stand the torch rested on, so I would always have a reminder of that day.

One of my friends was also honored to be a torchbearer. We agreed it was an incredible symbol of how we wanted to run our lives. For me, the torch meant that I was no longer standing still with CP.

For both of us, that Olympic torch said, "I have the power to accomplish anything I want."

**

Chapter 3

Growing Up In Aspen

I might have been dealt a challenging hand, but I've still had my share of aces. One of them is my family; another is my address. After all, not many people get to say they are a "true Aspenite." But I can.

Celebrity playground. Trendy mountain town. One of the world's most *chi chi* addresses. Take your pick. Aspen has been described in many ways. I don't think any of the major ones include "Home of Win Charles – up-and-coming artist challenged by cerebral palsy." But maybe some day Aspen will boast that title, too.

More seriously – and I am plenty serious about my future – I see the place where I live as a huge contributor to being the person I am today. Aspen has given me opportunities that I wouldn't have had otherwise. Aspen is a place for winners, and it has helped to make me a winner, too.

And I'm not the only one. It's important to me to point out that most of the kids I went to school with are true Aspenites, too. They are also winners. But we are a rare bunch. In a community of about 6,000 permanent residents, not many were born here. Nine out of ten people who live here now moved from either California or New York.

For those of us who are "Aspen certified," this has been a great place to grow up. As I think about all the ways Aspen shaped me, I am looking out the window of the house I grew up in. A milky winter haze has drifted over the landscape like a thin veil. Right now, I suspect that the winter glow goes far beyond my window and is covering the entire Roaring Fork Valley. The snow is scattered over a wide wooded lawn, as cozy and private as any secret garden.

This is the house my parents brought me to, after those anxious months that followed my birth. Given the enormous struggle it was for me just to come into the world, it's probably fitting that the house is in a secluded neighborhood. It gives me the freedom to decide how I will interact with the world. The nearest neighbors live somewhat of a trek distant – definitely not right next door. Since Mom passed away, I live here with Dad. The house is a reflection of our lives. Both of us are active, the kind of people who keep on keeping on.

Back in the 1970s, when Dad was around my age, he left the East Coast and Boston's refined urban setting. He wanted to stretch and test himself in the American West, which has always been a destination for figuring out one's dreams. As he built an audio business into a success, Dad also became an avid sportsman and skier. He has passed on to me that love of the outdoors.

But it wasn't always clear that I could do sports, indoor or outdoors.. As I work at my desk, I remember the many times I struggled as a child, whether to find my voice or to control my limbs. Back then, I would look out this very window and wonder what life had in store for me. The larger world beyond Aspen, and even Aspen itself, seemed so free! Would I ever be able to join it?

Now the question is being answered, and I am so grateful. But when I was just beginning to absorb all the opportunities that Aspen offered, I wasn't so certain.

Yet even then, I sensed that surprises awaited me. As a child, I was often startled by the various fascinating critters that paraded by. From my window, I saw deer, bears, and coyotes treat our backyard as their personal playground. The coyotes scared me the most, and I think it was due to that eerie aura they have. They do not seem gentle like deer, nor are they pudgy and deceptively cuddly like bears. Coyotes are sleek and nimble, with intense watchful eyes that are always scanning for prey. Their presence is unsettling.

While living in the Colorado backcountry, we learned to stay alert for wild animals. When I was about six years old, I was working at my desk one day when I suddenly became aware that something was watching me. The hairs on my neck stood up as I very slowly turned toward the window. There in the backyard stood a brown bear cub.

Cubs can look pudgy and awkward, but you don't live in even toney Aspen without having an appreciation of bear danger. Fascinated, I watched that cub, knowing that I was safe inside the house. And somehow I also knew that the brown bear was a promise of the bigger life that was waiting for me.

Get a Move On

Aspen is a strange mixture. We have wildlife in the backyard, but five minutes away there's an entirely different lifestyle. The great wild outdoors or urban chic – take your pick. There's constant bustle and an almost palpable energy in downtown Aspen.

On any given day, you might see jet-setters strolling down Main Street, wearing ultra-fashionable understated jeans and leather coats, and shaking off London and Paris time zones. Coming the other way might be young ski bums in jeans and warm-up jackets, just in from Denver for the weekend. A couple just up from sea level might be groggy as they adjust to Aspen's 8,000-foot elevation. While crossing the street, they're probably on the hunt for a coffee shop with the full-leaded stuff.

Few places, even out-of-the-way ones, have Aspen's diversity. Many people are surprised on their first visit. One look at the quaint Currier & Ives Main Street, and first-timers can't help saying, "Hey, this is a real town!"

In other words, Aspen is no Hollywood set. It might be a playground for the rich and famous, but it's also a cozy friendly place that in many ways still looks like Small Town, USA. The famous Hotel Jerome, where my parents met back in the 1970s, is on Main Street, which is four blocks from the gondola that takes winter skiers and summer hikers up the mountain.

When I was a kid, my goal was to get up that mountain. Of course, my limbs were imprisoned, my gait was halting, and my style was certainly not as fluid as Andy Mill's, a world-class skier who also grew up in Aspen. But despite the physical challenges, I wanted to learn how to ski, like my friends did. So I resolved to do it.

Dad thought it was a great idea. He was totally at home on the slopes, and he wanted to get me there, too. "Honey," he said, "you might be a bit slower than your friends, but you can do it!"

My parents had already given me a head start. They got me on the slopes when I was four years old.

I remember one particular day when we had lunch and then headed out for the mountain, to ski until 3 o'clock. My dad is an expert skier, and he planned to be my companion. Dad and some of his colleagues had collaborated to build a device that would let me become very adept on the slopes. It's an ingenious system – I'll tell you about it in a moment.

First I want to go on record with this. Much of my resolve and confidence on the slopes comes from the education I got at Aspen Country Day School. Country Day made me feel as if I could do anything. Right from the beginning, teachers and staff members encouraged me to make friends and be a part of whatever was going on.

One favorite memory is the school's physical education program. At Country Day, as soon as the first snow fell, we were on the slopes, learning to ski. Through 8th grade, my class went skiing every Thursday and Friday afternoon.. It was the best incentive for someone like me with huge physical challenges.

As privileged a place as Aspen is, the schools place a huge emphasis on helping those with tough challenges. During my high school years, I was involved in service clubs such as Outreach, which helps people with limited resources (yes, there are such people even in Aspen). The program is modeled on homeless shelters in Denver. It provides Christmas and holiday events and does other projects to brighten people's lives.

In high school, we all pitched in. I do not recall ever being asked to step aside, nor was I ever discounted or ignored because of my disability.

So I grew in confidence, in classrooms and outside them. Aspen is an excellent playground of the outdoors, and I took advantage of everything I could. At a young age, my classmates and I became hikers. I also became skilled at riding a recumbent bike, which accommodated my wayward limbs with their balance problems.

A body with cerebral palsy isn't exactly suited for a fast strenuous sport like skiing. My joints are stiff to begin with, and they often hurt outright. Add the stress of skiing and the cold temperature, and my joints are soon screaming, "Stop, stop!" So I had many physical challenges to face.

But I learned a valuable lesson from dealing with seemingly insurmountable challenges. If you are willing to ask for advice from others, to be creative and consider all options, it *is* possible to overcome almost anything.

Dad came up with an innovation that allowed me to ski. It was a vertical adaptive bar that fastened to my skis. I held onto this upright bar, which was both a stabilizer and a guide stick. Basically a walker on skis.

With that in place, I learned to ski.

By the time I was 16, I was quite good at it, and ready to move on to snowboarding. My generation prefers snowboarding, anyway. I happily discovered that for someone with CP, snowboarding is more natural and intuitive than skiing. I was also thrilled to find that the adaptive bar worked just as well on a snowboard.

But here's what's funny. When people saw me snowboarding down Aspen Mountain, they thought I was using a trick board. Cool! They had no idea that I was challenged with cerebral palsy. They thought I was an expert boarder who had invented a new technique!

Talk about a valuable lesson. Here you are, thinking you're in the toughest possible circumstance, yet other people are perceiving you as a winner.

I've been asked if I'm ever jealous of able-bodied people who effortlessly glide past me. Truthfully, the answer is no. I know that if I work hard enough, and do it enough times, I can do what an ordinary person can. I just do it differently. As with my adaptive snowboard, sometimes I even attract worthwhile attention.

It's like I'm opening doors of possibility for people who can't imagine themselves doing something difficult.

Today I'm in my mid-20s and very proud to be a "green" and a "blue" snowboarder. And I'm not talking bruises! I have conquered those slopes.

Or rather, on the slopes I conquered CP.

Getting Involved in Aspen Life

A black cloud loomed over me. The surgery in 2006 was supposed to give me more physical freedom. Instead, it took away much of the freedom I already had. It was a terrible setback in my athletic pursuits. It also made me very angry, but I resolved to overcome that, too.

The black cloud eventually dissipated and revealed some sunlight. My desire to overcome and move forward led to something good. Today I work with an organization called Challenge Aspen, an adaptive ski/snowboard program that was co-founded in 1995 by Amanda Boxtel (who is paralyzed) and Houston Cowan, an entrepreneur who doesn't take no for an answer.

As its website says, the organization's mission is to provide "meaningful recreational, educational, and cultural experiences to individuals faced with cognitive or physical challenges."

The words might be somewhat top heavy, but the organization is awesome. Challenge Aspen is now one of the world's best sports programs for disabled people.

I've also been motivated to push myself in other ways. Aspen is a Mecca of sports fitness, ability, and hardcore training. At the Aspen Club and Spa, I'm pushing myself in ways I never expected to. Four days a week I pull on leggings and a workout top, and I head for the club, where I have a yoga class with a private trainer. Yoga frees me from stiff joints and inflexible limbs.

Yoga has been found to be a huge benefit for people who are challenged by CP. From personal experience I know that's true. The Internet is alive with advice about bringing yoga into a daily routine. If you're challenged by CP, keep looking until you find a program that's right for you.

Then there's the Alter G – that stands for "alternative gravity." What a find! The device resembles a giant treadmill. It allows top athletes to train, and people with physical injuries or challenges to recover, by working out in virtual zero gravity. This is the device that gave me mobility. It juices stiff joints and allows me to feel nearly complete freedom.

I zip into a wetsuit-like contraption which fills up with air. Then I walk on the treadmill, free from 80 percent of my body weight. It's an amazing sensation even for the able-bodied. For someone who has to fight the drag of awkward flaying limbs, the sensation is incomparable.

The Alter G was originally designed for astronauts. It's a Space Age invention that turned out to have practical use for ordinary people in everyday life. It's an excellent solution for banged-up football players, injured skiers and snowboarders, celebrities with back sprains (many of them flock to Aspen), and for Win Charles, challenged by cerebral palsy.

I'm on the Alter G for thirty minutes at a time, three times a week. They are precious moments of freedom.

We have a small informal Alter G community now, people recovering from various things. One of my Alter G friends is paralyzed from the waist down. He skis on one ski, and does it as flexibly and as skillfully as any able-bodied skier. He does things on Aspen Mountain that many people would not do, because they're afraid or timid.

To me, this proves that many disabilities are in the mind. You could be "paralyzed" not by stiff unmoving limbs, but because your will and your determination are frozen. A frozen will dis-ables anyone from succeeding in life.

I've learned this important lesson in many ways and many places. Mom and Dad pushed me to be my best, whether I was learning to speak well or to ski down Aspen Mountain.

Aspen Country Day School encouraged me to contribute my individual strengths and to be my best at whatever I was doing. Challenge Aspen lets me meet remarkable competitors and athletes who know what real challenges are.

My friends have taught me that when you give your courage even a tiny nudge, you accomplish great things.

People Who Make a Difference

People ask me, "So do you have many celebrity friends in Aspen?" Well, I'm not impressed very much by celebrities. I'm drawn more to people who have overcome obstacles, or who meet challenges head on, and do something special with their lives.

One Aspen resident who deeply impresses me, and who I count as a friend, is Chris Klug. He is the only person in the U.S. to survive a liver transplant and then win an Olympic medal. As a matter of fact, some of the proceeds of this book will go to the Chris Klug Foundation, a nonprofit which spreads the powerful message of organ donation. The procedure saved Chris's life and allowed him to remain in the sports world and to compete.

Chris's story is amazing. He was born in Denver (but we forgive him for that!), and became one of the world's best snowboarders. In 2000 he needed a liver transplant. Two years later, after the transplant, he competed in the Olympics and won a Bronze Medal. Shortly after that awesome accomplishment, Chris started the foundation. He has won more awards in World Cup competitions.

There are many unsung heroes in Aspen. Every time I return to Aspen Country Day School, where I spent my school years from pre-school through 8th grade, I think of two people in particular.

I've been working at the school since 2010; for me, it's a privilege and an unexpected blessing. Every day when I gaze across the campus pond, I recall how it was my classmates' favorite ice-skating rink. Thanks to two teachers who encouraged me, I've skated on that pond, too.

Shelly was my kindergarten teacher, and Susi taught me in the first grade. In the days before the Americans with Disabilities Act, the school, like many institutions, was pretty quirky in its handicap-friendly access. Shelly and Susi were especially kind and attentive as I was wheeled across truck ramps and over rough pathways.

More than once I got slammed on my face when the chair tipped over while it was being pushed by a zealous driver.

It has always amazed me that kids are usually gentler drivers than adults.

Shelly and Susi both coaxed me to be a good reader and keep up with the rest of the class. That was difficult because I didn't have good verbal skills, and it was hard for me just to hold a book. But these wonderful teachers would say, "Let's see what Win can do. If she can't manage it, we'll modify. But we won't let Win down!"

Remembering moments like those makes me cry. These teachers helped shape me into the person I am today. They pushed me toward my full potential.

Now that I'm a full-time aide at the school, it feels strange to be Susi's and Shelly's colleague. My former teachers sometimes tease me by showing the current kids photos of me as a child. They tell the children that they knew me "way back when."

That's pretty weird. But it's pretty wonderful, too.

**

Chapter 4

Living with a Disability in a Normal World

I always joke that God "blessed" me with cerebral palsy. What I mean is that I have learned many things, and understood many more, that I would never have had a chance to experience without CP in my life.

I'm blessed because no matter how many or large my needs were, my family had the financial, physical, and emotional resources to take care of me. Whether they were spending all day in the Neonatal Intensive Care Unit, spending hours in prayer, or waiting for me to come out of surgery, my parents were always determined to see me through.

It might seem to an outsider that since I was born with cerebral palsy, my family gave me everything I wanted. But that would be a huge misconception. My family took care of me extremely well, but I had to work hard, too, to get the fabulous life I wanted.. It took both hard physical work (by me) and huge emotional work by all of us in my family.

I was blessed to have a normal childhood despite the CP disability, and I'm sure that has framed my thoughts about what my life should be like. I grew up surrounded by able-bodied people in Aspen, and I saw no reason that I shouldn't do what they did, even if I had to do it differently.

No one told me, "No, Win, you can't do that, you have CP." Instead, they found a way that would allow me to do the things I really wanted, and to accomplish the goals we all set for me. After many years of learning that I really can do many things, I'm more determined than ever to find ways to reach the other goals I have.

My entire education from kindergarten through 12th grade was with friends who were not disabled. I have many wonderful memories, but my favorite school memory is skiing with my classmates on Thursday and Friday afternoons. It was a perfect example of how I *could* do what everyone did, only a little bit differently.

Some adults created a walker on skis for me. Not only was the walker on skis, but I was on skis in the middle of the walker. It was an amazing contraption that worked wonderfully. The walker frame provided the extra stability I needed. I used the device for over ten years, then for two years I was able to ski without it. When I was sixteen, I gave up skiing for a new sport that all my friends were doing. It's called snowboarding, and it is totally fun.

We had to figure out how I could snowboard with a disability. The sport was so new that no one had yet developed any helpful snowboard devices. But in the Adaptive Ski Program (part of Challenge Aspen, where I still ski every weekend), we came up with an adaptive snowboard.

As I mentioned, my board looks like a trick board. The only difference between it and the other boards out there is that my board has a bar attached to it, and I hang onto the bar. It works very well. Every winter I still enjoy snowboarding.

Another wonderful school memory is participating in school plays at Aspen Country Day School. When I was attending Country Day (up to the 8th grade), I loved to act in the plays they put on. If I wasn't in a play, I was watching it.

I also have many good travel memories. Despite having a disability, I have been a world traveler and have thoroughly enjoyed the trips. Of all the places I visited, my four favorites are Russia, Alaska, Amsterdam, and Sweden, . My all-time best memory is from when we visited the Hermitage in St. Petersburg, Russia, and I was allowed to touch the paintings. I love art, so I'm an avid museum visitor. I constantly want to immerse myself in all forms of art.

When I was seven years old, my family took a cruise to Alaska that included a port stop in Sitka. We flew over glacial ice in a helicopter, and the views were fabulous. We also stood on that same ice when we visited the town. The most impressive thing about the cruise, though, was that the ship actually looked bigger than the town!

My 13th birthday is also a fabulous memory because I got to spend the day at the Van Gogh Art Museum in the Netherlands. For a girl who loves art, this was not only fun but educational, too, in a surprising way. Even though the museum is named for the famous artist and has five floors altogether, it uses only two floors to display the art that Vincent Van Gogh created. It was pretty wonderful anyway!

Other parts of the Netherlands that I love to recall are the beautiful tulip fields and watching all the cool windmills in action.

I think, though, the absolute best of all my travel experiences was cruising through the Panama Canal. Hearing the background story of the Canal while watching the locks opening and closing was storytelling made memorable. It was more meaningful than if I'd read a textbook. Learning history while traveling is way more fun than classroom learning.

My house at the beach has always been a favorite place, too. I love the ocean, even though I can't swim or even walk on the beach normally. Instead, I do what I call Ocean Walking. I'm not sure that anyone else walks on the beach or in the water quite like I do. Once again I have adapted as I need to for this particular disability.

When I walk along the shoreline, two people, one on each side of me, support me against the ocean current. Walking in the water this way takes pressure off some of my joints.

At first, this might seem easier than walking against gravity, but it sure isn't. I wait until high tide, then I walk in the sand, which moves with the current. This walk really uses all my muscles, and is great exercise as well as enjoyable.

I don't usually do the Ocean Walk on a public beach with hundreds of people coming and going. But at our beach house in the Bahamas, I love to walk at a private inlet, where I can also look back on a pink stucco house with a white tile roof.

People ask me, "Win, why don't you go swimming in a pool?" It's true that when you live in Colorado, a swimming pool is much easier to find than an ocean beach is. Not much beach access in the mountains.

But for me, there are usually too many people in a swimming pool, and because of CP, I'm a bit uneasy in crowds. If people are playing hard and not paying attention to others around them, I feel on edge. It's too easy for me to get knocked off balance. It feels much safer for me to go in the ocean and just walk.

After my back operation in 2006, the physical therapist asked me to swim in the pool, as a way of getting my muscles back in shape with the least stress on them. Being in the pool was good physical therapy, but I didn't really enjoy it because it wasn't the ocean. However, much more than I like a swimming pool, I do enjoy a hot tub.

I'm laughing as I write this because when it comes right down to it, I'm also a germ-a-phobe! As a disabled but healthy person who doesn't want to get sick or be injured, I feel that walking in the ocean is my safest and healthiest choice.

Because of my disability, my body has had many broken bones. I've even had some bones broken in the operating room so doctors could straighten them, so I would have a better chance at living the life I want to live.

I've also had two really frightening operations. The first was open heart surgery, but I don't remember it, because I was only weeks old. Naturally it was most scary for my parents.

At the time of the second surgery, I was 18 years old, so I remember quite a bit. That was the operation on my back that left me mobile only with the use of a walker.

When I woke up after surgery, I asked the nurse, "What hospital is this? Why am I here?" It was midnight, and I could hear rain. I could hear medical equipment beeping. A brown-haired nurse standing by the hospital bed calmly told me, "You're in Children's Hospital, and you just had back surgery." I had no idea what day it was, I was on so much pain medication. Frankly, I didn't even remember going in for surgery the day before.

"No wonder I hurt so much," I told the nurse. I still remember that traumatic time. And I remember how grateful I am for having grown up in Aspen where I got the good medical care that allows me to be mobile and strong enough to write this book.

Some of you might be wondering if my friends ever teased me as I was growing up. Kids being what they are, it's amazing but true that no one ever did tease me about being disabled. As I get older, I'm thinking that it might have something to do with growing up in a small town like Aspen, rather than in a large impersonal city like Denver.

I went to elementary school with people who are still my good friends now. Several former high school classmates remain my friends as well. Aspen is a small community, and in many ways is more friendly and supportive than a big city. My parents and my teachers were all supportive and they set a good example for my classmates and friends to follow.

When I was real young, I didn't go to sleepovers at friends' houses, as many kids do. And I didn't have play dates, either. But the cool thing my parents did was to plan a fabulous birthday bash for me every year.

Since my birthday is in the summer, my parents went all out. They invited all my friends and we had an all-day party. The main event would be from noon to maybe 4 o'clock. My mom would set up all sorts of exciting activities for the kids, then we'd have a picnic lunch under a tent in the backyard. My parents made it so much fun!

As I got older I wanted smaller and more intimate parties. For my 12th birthday, my parents planned a party at the cooking school, and I could invite only a few people. It was hard to decide who to invite. The bar was so high that everyone in my class wanted to come. They all thought we threw the best birthday parties.

One day before my birthday I was walking down a tree-lined path at Country Day. I was with a friend who asked me, "Win, can I come to your birthday party?" I had to tell her that it was at the cooking school that year instead of at our house. She said, "Win, you have the best birthday parties and I want to come!" And I felt so good.

Despite my disability, my friends have been very supportive of me. They don't seem to see me as a disabled person. Whether disabled or not, we all need supportive friends in order to live the most fabulous life we want and are striving for.

By living life to the fullest, we can all enjoy each moment of every day.

**

Chapter 5

Attending College

Some people are very surprised that I went to college, but completing a four-year degree has always been one of my dreams. At this point, I have a two-year degree in Early Childhood Education from a community college, and I am working toward a baccalaureate degree. I have set myself a schedule for completing that degree, and I'm working hard to accomplish it.

Eventually I'd like a job teaching art, and right now, I need more credentials to make that happen. My mother passed away before she saw me get a two-year degree, but it brought me comfort to remember how she supported me throughout my educational journey.

Like every other challenge, I met college head on. It certainly wasn't easy. Being a college freshman is hard enough for an able-bodied person, but it's ten times harder for someone with cerebral palsy. I had to take two college reading classes just to be admitted. I went to summer school, then took an Independent Study class with a tutor who was also a professor at Colorado Mountain College (CMC). It was not the most fun summer I've ever had, but it did prepare me for college entrance.

CMC also required that I take a entrance test to make sure I was ready for the next level. Most people take the test once, but I took it three times before I was admitted.

The second required reading class was in Glenwood with kids who all had disabilities. The teacher covered the material quite slowly so that everyone could understand. Quite frankly, that drove me up the wall. Amazingly, my brain has rewired itself over the years, so I think very much like someone who isn't disabled. *Slow* is just not how I think.

The reading class gave me an idea of what college classes could be like. A story I like to tell about it is called "The Vocab Book." When the class began, the teacher gave us a vocabulary book. Since it was the beginning of the semester, I expected the book to be an introduction to the formal work of getting an education degree.

But when I met with my tutor, she took one look at it and said, "Win, this is the wrong vocabulary book for this class." I said the teacher herself had handed it out.

My tutor and I were both shocked – the teacher had ordered the wrong book. The class was supposed to be level two. That introduction to college life let me know right away that even at college level, teachers are people, too.

The class was also on a real college campus, which I liked. Finally I felt that I was truly on my way.

To get my degree, I also took an education summer class with able-bodied students. The professor was in Vail, so class was held on the CMC video system. It's called IVS for Interactive Video System. Microphones and cameras are set up so you can hear and see the professor, and she can see and hear the students.

There's a button that opens and closes the mike, and sometimes students forgot to turn it off, so everyone else heard all the side conversations. Sometimes it was entertaining, but I'm very thankful that no one discussed my disability when they thought they weren't being overheard.

Including me, there were only ten people in the IVS class. It was in the CMC video room which was in the basement next to a dance studio. I hated taking classes in that tiny room. I much preferred to attend classes in person. Of course, even better are the on-line courses you can take while wearing your PJs.

A really cool thing about the summer class was that my aide and I got along really well. She was the only other student from Aspen. The class was "Teaching the Exceptional Preschooler," It taught us how to deal with both disabled preschoolers and gifted and talented kids. When we got to a lesson on cerebral palsy, the prof asked me to share my first-hand knowledge. I loved that part, sharing my personal experiences of CP.

Because my disability sometimes makes me slow at answering questions, the college handled test-taking differently for me. I took the same tests the other students did, but I was granted a time extension. The head of the CMC Special Education Department gave me a note to give to the class professor, so I would be allowed extra time for the test.

Let me tell you, some tests were not easy for able-bodied people, much less for me! At some point most college students cry about difficult tests. I sure did.

But I kept working on the material, because I was very determined to get a degree.

The rest of the classes I took for an education degree were in the fall and the winter. Like most students, I hated taking classes in the summer or at night. Since the summer IVS class was in the basement at CMC, there were no windows from which I could watch the sun set. To me, it's the best part of the day, the part I truly enjoy.

The way the semester schedule was at CMC, there was only one week between the winter and summer semesters, and another week between summer and fall semesters. That year, I had only two weeks of summer.

I'm surprised that my parents and family members in the Bahamas let me do that, but since the classes I needed were only offered at those times, I didn't have much choice. If I think about it now, I know I learned a lot. But it might have been better to slow down a bit and enjoy the summer, rather than rushing to get my degree.

On the other hand, I've wanted to teach from the time I was quite young. I very much wanted a degree in Education,. In elementary and middle school, I saw how much love my teachers gave me. They truly inspired me to do the same for others.

By the time I was a sophomore in high school, I had a tentative plan for what to do with the rest of my life. And by that time, I also knew that what I wanted would be a serious challenge, just like high school was. Since I was disabled, I could receive services from the Special Education Department at my high school until I was 21, if I so desired.

But I respectfully declined more assistance, and made up my mind to get an education degree at CMC.

While going to college, I was also volunteering in the education field, so I could get my foot in the door soon after graduation. My first year of teaching at the Aspen District Preschool was in 2006, then I took a year off from college to let my back recover from surgery.

A friend was kind enough to recommend me for the volunteer job.

Working on a degree and at the same time having a job in that field complement each other. At the beginning of each semester, the professor would ask us students how many of us already had teaching jobs. That let the professor know what subjects to focus on and what assignments to give out. In all the teaching classes I took, there were practical hands-on assignments in the classroom. These were based on the lesson we'd be learning in class the next week.

My next class was about making lesson plans for preschoolers. It was taught by a woman from Leadville who looked to me like a mini version of Sarah Palin, with the same voice inflections. She was a mom who would have preferred to be at home with her kids on Tuesday nights when we had class. To this day, I think the teacher did not understand that I was disabled. The class was not one of my better college experiences.

Yes, even in college there's homework. There's an on-line system called Blackboard, which mimics an actual high school blackboard. The professor puts questions on these discussion boards, and students answer them. We scored points for answering correctly, and we also accumulated points for being present and answering questions at all. This system was used in both the IVS and other on-line classes.

I remember telling the professor in Leadville that I had to miss a week of class for a trip to the Bahamas. For quite a while, our family vacation was scheduled at that time. But since I also really wanted to take the class, I was hoping to work around the missed time and do some makeup work later.

When the professor asked me the reason for the trip, and I told her it was a family vacation, she said, "Be sure to take laptop and books with you to the Caribbean."

Then she added that if I didn't do the assignments while I was on vacation, she would give me an F for the semester.

Carrying a large laptop through an airport is not easy for anyone, not to mention carrying a heavy textbook, too. I probably looked like a mad woman. When I go through airport security, they usually make me sit in the wheelchair while they pat it down. Then I have to take off my shoes, just like everyone else.

Fortunately, a TSA agent takes me through the gate for handicapped people. Maybe a woman in a yellow wheelchair looks like she could have a bomb with her, but I sure don't feel like a terrorist. That time, going through security took extra time because I had the laptop with me.

You who have traveled know that everyone who carries a laptop onto a plane first has to take it out of the bag so security can swipe it down. Since I'm not very fast in my movements, you can imagine the furor I caused when I did this just as everyone else was rushing through security at the same time. But I've traveled enough by now to know the routine pretty well when it comes to wheelchairs and security.

I couldn't forget the heavy textbook in my carry-on, which my mother told the guard was hers. The security guard looked at Mom like she had two heads, but at that point I didn't care. We needed to get through security as quickly as possible.

When I look back at that situation, I'm surprised that I didn't end up on the floor with the laptop and the heavy textbook on top of me.

In the Bahamas I had to tell my family that I wasn't just on vacation that week, that I also had some college assignments to do. Of course, they already knew I was in college, because I had made previous arrangements for someone to help me read the text.

Doing the homework assignment with a laptop and in the Bahamas was no easy feat.

Besides the distractions – uh, I mean, good reasons for not studying – there was that wonderful ocean view. I remember looking out at the ocean with the laptop in front of me, trying to figure out why I had gotten such a low score on a Blackboard question the night before. From the Bahamas, I called the Special Ed department head at CMC, asking her to find out why the low score. She never answered my question, and I never figured it out.

That vacation week, I read every afternoon. It sure wasn't fun sitting inside, reading a college textbook while I was so near the beach. I personally would have chosen almost any other book except a textbook, but I did read it. One night I locked myself in the downstairs den just to answer a question on the Blackboard. It was very hard to stay motivated when the weather was so wonderful and the ocean was just a few steps away.

But I really wanted that degree, so I buckled down and studied. And it was worth it, because the professor didn't give me an F for taking a week off and going to the Bahamas!

The next college class I took was at the elementary school in Basalt, a few miles downvalley from Aspen. It was taught by a nice woman named Kay. This class was in person, not on-line. Kay was a retired teacher who talked to us about the well-being of preschoolers.

The really cool thing about the class was that it was full of women with different teaching backgrounds and very different teaching styles. Some of the students already taught at the Wildwood School (another private school in Aspen). I loved hearing their stories about Wildwood. At the end of each class, Kay had story time for the teachers and *by* the teachers. The stories were so interesting that we never got out of class on time.

The next two classes were about preschool safety. The first one, held in a CMC classroom in Aspen, was the hardest I've ever taken. It was not only physically challenging to do CPR on a doll, it was also emotionally challenging as we listened to stories and watched videos about child abuse. I learned a lot in that class, but I sure didn't enjoy it.

The second of the two-part series was taught on-line by a man named Mark. The class was about "stranger danger" and how to teach preschoolers about it, so they would understand enough to remain safe. To be honest, as a disabled woman, I also needed that information.

Now I'm laughing as I write. It's funny that the "stranger danger" information is meant not only for preschoolers, but for this teacher, too. So much of what I learned, I can use in my personal life as well as in a career of teaching preschoolers.

In fact, it's useful for everyone. One of the saddest things I learned in that class was the signs of child abuse. I wish it just didn't happen, so we wouldn't have to be trained to watch for it.

If you have never taken an on-line class, you might think it's the easiest thing in the world. But in different ways, it can be just as difficult as a class you attend in person. You still do lots of homework, and you have to wait just as long to have it graded. And on-line tests don't give you instant results, either. You also wait for them to be graded.

When I answered questions posted on Blackboard, it took about a week for Mark to grade them. My biggest fear was always that my Mac had eaten my homework!

I did have a tutor to help me. She herself was taking the class, and was a supervisor at the Aspen School District where I was working at the time. Besides getting an education in the on-line class, I learned a little about the supervisor's personal life. At the time, her minor child was sleeping under a bridge with a homeless man, while the supervisor didn't seem all that worried about it. It certainly made for some interesting times.

The final class I took to qualify for a degree was the History of Education. It covered various educational philosophies.

All in all, I found college totally fascinating. I met many different people from all walks of life. Now I'm looking forward to the classes I'll be taking to earn a four-year degree.

**

Chapter 6

Working with a Disability

Even though I have a disability, I still need to work. It's for the obvious monetary reasons, of course, but it's also for my mental health. I need to feel productive and useful just like everyone else does. If you are wondering what job I could hold as a physically disabled woman, the answer might surprise you. I not only have one job; I currently have three.

My first job is being an artist. I've mentioned that I started a company for my artwork. After I publish this book, I'm going to spend time on making Aspen Rose Arts a really good company. I don't have an art studio – I wish I did – that's something I can look forward to.

Right now all my art is created digitally with a computer program on my Mac. I take photographs and digitally rework, combine, and enhance them, until they look like oil paintings. Each piece of art I create takes about two hours to complete. I sell my artwork on-line at various places such as Zazzle and Redbubble. First I upload a digital image, then the physical work of making posters or cards is handled for the artist. That way, I can concentrate on things I do well (creating art), and can let them do the rest.

I love creating my paintings. I can't imagine life without this particular joy. I create art almost daily. It relaxes me so much and that keeps me in a happy and confident frame of mind. When I complete a painting, I feel both elated and satisfied in a way that's hard to describe. I intend to keep creating and adding to my body of work for a long time, because I can't imagine anything else that gives me such joy and fulfillment.

While I'm promoting my art, some fun things happen. I get photos of celebrities holding my artwork. After my mother died, I got a very cool picture of Taylor Armstrong from the TV show *The Real Housewives of Beverly Hills*. Now I have quite a few photographs with my artwork in other celebrities' hands as well.

After Mom died, I was so very sad about losing her, and unsure what to do next. She had always been right beside me, helping me organize my thoughts about my art, then actually helping me promote it. One day I got on Facebook and thought, *What am I going to do now to promote my art?* That's when I found a wonderful group called the indiExhibit.

For a membership fee, the founders of indiExhibit take my artwork, along with the work of about one hundred other artists, to private VIP suites at events such as the Oscars and the Emmys. Taylor Armstrong was holding my artwork at the Sundance Film Festival in Utah.

The photo of Taylor Armstrong holding my artwork is most special to me because it was my very first show. The excitement and suspense are extreme, because the artist is never sure exactly which celebrities will come to an event, or which ones will choose to be photographed with the art. By now I've sent my artwork across the country many times, and the excitement is still there.

My artwork has even been featured in the *LA Times*, and that was thrilling, too. The funniest thing about it, though, was that I didn't know it was in the paper until someone in the indiExhibit posted a link. I went to the page to congratulate all the artists who were pictured there, and lo and behold, there was a picture of my own artwork! I was stunned and thrilled at the same time.

There's another way I share my artwork. I have now self-published three books about my work. One of them is what Taylor Armstrong was holding in the photo.

Now I'm laughing again – publishing an art book is certainly easier than publishing an autobiography!

My second job is being a Stella and Dot jewelry representative. The company's website calls it, "an *Inc. 500 fastest-growing company* ... a San Francisco based social selling company ... creates flexible entrepreneurial opportunities for women.

"Our boutique-style jewelry and accessories line is available exclusively through in-home Trunk Shows by Independent Stylists and on-line. Our one-of-a-kind collections are designed by celebrated New York designers and featured in *Gossip Girl*, *In Style*, and *Lucky Magazine*, as well as on the wrists and necklines of today's hottest celebrities.

"*The Today Show*, *Wall Street Journal*, and *The New York Times* have all praised Stella and Dot for our innovative social shopping concept which brings together the best of e-commerce, social media, personal service, and passionate earning to create the ultimate home-based business for today's modern woman."

I love this second job, too. It's very possible to do this kind of selling as a disabled person. If you've been looking for an opportunity, this is definitely worth checking into.

I can't forget that I also have a teaching job that I get up for every morning. I'm finally being paid to teach, and the job is in a field that I'd hoped to get into when I got my education degree.

I have many stories from teaching, some wonderful, some not so. One great thing is hearing the kids call me "Miss Wid" instead of "Miss Win" because at age three, most kids can't say "N" in that cute kid voice.

As I reflect on it, I realize that I really love to teach. And like most other teachers, no, I didn't go into it for the money.

When I first got a teaching job back in 2006, I was referred by a friend. I was so excited to get anything in the education field that I didn't care whether it was a volunteer thing or a paid job. At the time I didn't need to work for money, so anything in teaching was OK with me.

I probably should have hung on a little longer and waited for the paid job I have now. Even though my boss was super-nice the first year, the whole experience could have been better. But I was impatient, of course, and just wanted to get started, so I jumped at the chance to do anything in the education field.

As part of that first job, I went to conferences of the National Educational Association of Young Children (NEAYC). The trips weren't always trouble-free. Sometimes I was uneasy when I traveled. Because of my disability, I often need an aide to help me on a trip.

One particular trip had quite an impact. Apparently the aide was taking anti-depressant medication, and also liked to drink. Most people know that this is not a great combination. I was forced to rely on someone whose life was in turmoil. I wasn't aware of this until we had settled into a nice suite in Dallas, and she surprised me by joking that if she didn't take her mediation, she might get "wonky" on me.

I was not at all amused. The situation was definitely worrisome to someone who needs a caregiver! Luckily for both of us, the trip went all right, but I have never forgotten the need to be very careful about who I choose to help me with daily tasks.

The volunteer job went all right for about a year, but as many jobs do, it then took a downturn. I became disenchanted with both the work and management, and pretty unhappy with my situation. When the supervisor decided to open a new preschool in Aspen, it was time for me to take a break.

One day I went home, stood on the stairs, and announced to Mom that I'd *had* it! I was done with teaching. Always supportive, Mom said that if I was tired of teaching, maybe I should concentrate on creating artwork. I could start my own company and see how I liked being my own boss for a while.

That was an excellent idea, I decided, so we made plans for my new business. Of course I had no idea that my mom would pass away that summer, and that I would be left feeling even more uncertain about what direction to take my life in.

When Mom died, I assumed I would go back to the teacher's aide job. But while I was with Mom in the hospital, a voice came into my heart and my head. It sounded much like the principal of Country Day School.

The voice said, "You don't need to go back to that stressful teaching job. You need to come *here* where we will love and support you and help you through the grief about your mom."

Having learned to listen to my heart in many matters, ten days after my mom died I applied for a job as a teaching aide at Aspen Country Day School. I was hired, and this is the job I have today. I still love the work and the people I work with.

For the first year, I was in the classroom two days a week and in the office one day a week. Then the office manager decided they needed me in the office more, to help with the paperwork. But after a while, everyone realized that I loved the preschool children and they loved me, and that we learned so much from each other.

So I went back into the classroom. It provides consistency for both me and the children as we learn together about life and love.

**

Chapter 7

Keeping a Disabled Superwoman Healthy

I want to dispel a myth that seems to surround people with cerebral palsy. Many able-bodied people think that those with CP gain weight because they sit around all day, not doing anything.

But the actual truth is that people with CP have a considerably higher metabolism than most people do. As I write this book, I'm burning more than 100 calories an hour. Just to remain sitting upright is a tremendous effort for people with CP.

Besides regular speaking, I also speak into Siri, Apple's speech-to-text application, which means that as odd as it sounds, when I write I must project my voice, and that takes even more energy. All in all, it's not very difficult for me to stay slender.

You see, cerebral palsy is not just a neurological condition; it also affects the skeleton. Left on its own, my body tends to curl up in a tight ball. To prevent this, I have to stretch every day, to keep muscles and tendons from getting tight where they shouldn't be.

For example, because my hamstrings are really tight and my hip flexers are very weak, I have to train like an athlete just to be reasonably mobile. Exercising seven days a week certainly burns enough calories to keep me slim!

Three days a week I go to the gym to use the Alter G (the "alternate gravity" machine) which is a treadmill attached to an air bag. I get on it while wearing shorts that are like a wetsuit. I zip myself into the bag, and then it fills up with air. At the beginning of the air fill, my personal trainer holds me down, because I'm a *skinny Minnie* and don't weigh enough to stay down on my own. It's quite an experience!

In the summer I bike all over town. You might be wondering how anyone with CP could ride a bike; it just doesn't seem possible at first. But I'm lucky to have a candy-apple red, hot-looking three-wheeled recumbent bike. When I'm riding it, I don't look at all disabled. I love it!

I'm even allowed to ride it on the Cooper and Hyman malls in Aspen, although there are rules against bike riding on the malls. But the recumbent bike helps me maintain strength and mobility. It's similar to what a "seeing eye" dog does for a blind person who can take the animal into a restaurant or on a bus.

During the summer I want to get out and bike every day, because I really enjoy a good ride. Quite frankly, it could be a bit dangerous for a disabled person to ride a bike, so I make sure to avoid heavy traffic areas like Main Street.

Of course, there's all those wondering looks I get as I ride through town, especially at the Saturday Market. People sometimes ask me things about my bike, or they just admire it (and maybe me, too). "What a cool bike!"

It makes me happy to hear that, especially when I'm doin' wheelies on my candy-apple-red bike!

My other favorite sport is a winter one... snow-boarding. It's good exercise, and fun, too. And I don't fall very often. I feel blessed that I live in an area where this choice is available to me.

Once a week I do yoga and get a massage, to help my body stay as fit as it can be. But you know what? The very best exercise – for me as for most people – is to walk. It's not good for any body to stay immobile for very long. Of course I use a walker now, another great assistive device.

If you think you can't work out or do any exercising because you're disabled, that might not be true. At least it's worth checking into.

Living in Aspen makes me feel doubly blessed. There are so many ways to stay slim here. Because of the town's elevation (7,908 feet), you rarely see overweight people in Aspen. The body has to work harder at high elevations, so it uses more calories just to exist.

And people who live here or vacation here tend to be very health conscious. The fact that a disabled person works out at a gym doesn't surprise anyone – practically the whole town is into workouts. Quite a few people I know are in wheelchairs, and they also work out to keep their muscles strong and pliable. It's just part of the Aspen lifestyle.

**

Chapter 8

Today

I'm not afraid of storms, for I'm learning
to sail my ship.
Louisa May Alcott

You might be wondering why a disabled woman would write a book in the first place. One of my dreams has been to share my story with the world.

From May 2011 to June 2012, I attended a leadership workshop for the disabled. It was held one Saturday a month, at the Third Street Center in Carbondale, Colorado. The workshop was called "Taking Charge," and its focus was not necessarily on how to deal with a disability, but on how to be a better person in your own life.

At the workshop's beginning, the participants were asked to share their dreams in a meeting held later that month. I came up with ten dreams to share!

The leadership workshop inspired me. On May 8, 2011, in front of eleven people, I shared my dreams and presented my goals. One of them was to write this book.

I've had many problems with writing it. When I first started, a writing team in Denver was helping me. But after only three chapters were done, the team notified me by e-mail that they were quitting my project.

I can still remember the devastating e-mail I got, just before I went to yoga class that day. The personal touch of a phone call would have been kinder and preferable.

That day I didn't tell the yoga teacher that my book was figuratively falling apart. It probably was not smart to hire someone I found on Google, who was based in Denver, instead of getting a referral from someone I trusted and who was closer to home. I was simply too anxious to get started on my big project.

With only three chapters done and no other writer on the horizon, the publishing date had to be pushed back. As it turned out, though, so many people knew that I was writing a book that within 72 hours of the writing team's exit e-mail, my friends and family had found referrals for me.

That's how I got in contact with a super-great organization called the Aspen Writers Foundation. There I was given referrals to various writers, but at the time, no one was available for what I needed.

Then with help from the AWF Tuesday night writers workshop, where all levels and styles of writing are welcome, I met a phenomenal editor named LINELLE.

I also met with a friend (Margaret Bender) who had published a book titled "From Grief to Celebration." And we met with the person who helped with her book. Margaret's editor told me, "Win, at this point, it will be easier for *you* to write the book than to find a writer."

So on May 21, 2011, I started dictating to Siri. For those who aren't familiar with Siri, "she" is Apple's speech dictation application for the iPhone. If you have the time, Siri can definitely write your book.

Now that I think about it, there aren't many books written on the iPhone. But whatever the method I've used, it has been quite therapeutic for me, helping me deal with grief over losing my mother and also the challenge of putting my thoughts down on paper.

This is something I needed to do for myself and for all the adults who don't know about or understand my disability. Writing this has been fun for me personally.

Now I'm planning to write another book to teach children about this disability. That might be even more fun than writing for adults.

I am a disabled woman living a non-disabled life. I hope you will join me in the next chapter of my journey.

**

ABOUT THE AUTHOR

I, Win Charles, was born in 1987 in Aspen,
Colorado, where I still live.

I am a self-taught artist who became interested in art
as a way to cope with cerebral palsy.
The medium I use most often is digital art.

Besides life in general, I am artistically inspired by roses
and orchids, and the flora and fauna of the Bahamas.
The Bahaman people are also wonderful inspirations
for me – I truly admire them.

**

ABOUT THE EDITOR

LINELLE is a former librarian who turned
to writing and editing as a logical extension
of her "jack of all trades" background.

She currently works and lives happily in Aspen,
where she feels like she is on top of the world.
She hopes that the last thing she sees
before she leaves Mother Earth
will be the glorious mountains.

**

Made in the USA
Lexington, KY
10 November 2012

At age 24 I decided to tell my story.

Writing this autobiography gave me the opportunity to pay tribute to my family members who are passionate about life and have instilled this passion in me. My parents extraordinary support, encouragment, and pure love were my foundation as I navigated life, overcame obstacles,and achieved successes as a young woman with cerebral palsy.

I have to pay full tribute to my mother, who died in August 2010. From her I learned to listen to my own voice as a guide to making life choices. She taught me to always expect the best from myself.

My hope is that this book will provide insight into the extraordinary possibilities that those who live with disabilities have.I also hope that those without disabilities rather than putting a focus on our differences will come to understand what we all have in common.

This book is for my mom – with love.